WITHDRAWN

ABRAHAM LINCOLN

The Presidents of the United States

George Washington
1789–1797

John Adams
1797–1801

Thomas Jefferson
1801–1809

James Madison
1809–1817

James Monroe
1817–1825

John Quincy Adams
1825–1829

Andrew Jackson
1829–1837

Martin Van Buren
1837–1841

William Henry Harrison
1841

John Tyler
1841–1845

James Polk
1845–1849

Zachary Taylor
1849–1850

Millard Fillmore
1850–1853

Franklin Pierce
1853–1857

James Buchanan
1857–1861

Abraham Lincoln
1861–1865

Andrew Johnson
1865–1869

Ulysses S. Grant
1869–1877

Rutherford B. Hayes
1877–1881

James Garfield
1881

Chester Arthur
1881–1885

Grover Cleveland
1885–1889

Benjamin Harrison
1889–1893

Grover Cleveland
1893–1897

William McKinley
1897–1901

Theodore Roosevelt
1901–1909

William H. Taft
1909–1913

Woodrow Wilson
1913–1921

Warren Harding
1921–1923

Calvin Coolidge
1923–1929

Herbert Hoover
1929–1933

Franklin D. Roosevelt
1933–1945

Harry Truman
1945–1953

Dwight Eisenhower
1953–1961

John F. Kennedy
1961–1963

Lyndon Johnson
1963–1969

Richard Nixon
1969–1974

Gerald Ford
1974–1977

Jimmy Carter
1977–1981

Ronald Reagan
1981–1989

George H. W. Bush
1989–1993

William J. Clinton
1993–2001

George W. Bush
2001–2009

ABRAHAM LINCOLN

BILLY ARONSON

Marshall Cavendish
Benchmark
New York

Marshall Cavendish Benchmark
99 White Plains Road
Tarrytown, New York 10591-5502
www.marshallcavendish.us

All Internet addresses were correct at the time of printing.

Library of Congress Cataloging-in-Publication Data

Aronson, Billy.
Abraham Lincoln / by Billy Aronson
p. cm. — (Presidents and their times)
Summary: "Provides comprehensive information on President Abraham Lincoln and places him
within his historical and cultural context. Also explored are the formative events of his times and how
he responded"—Provided by publisher.
Includes bibliographical references and index.
ISBN 978-0-7614-2839-8
1. Lincoln, Abraham, 1809–1865—Juvenile literature. 2. Presidents—United States—Biography—
Juvenile literature. 3. United States—History—Civil War, 1861–1865—Juvenile literature. I. Title.
E457.905.A765 2008
973.7092—dc22
[B]   2007019190

Editor: Christine Florie
Publisher: Michelle Bisson
Art Director: Anahid Hamparian
Series Designer: Alex Ferrari

Photo research by Connie Gardner

Cover photo by Abraham Lincoln (1809–65) 1864 (coloured engraving) American School (19th century)
Private Collection. Peter Newark American Pictures/The Bridgeman Art Library.

The photographs in this book are used by permission and through the courtesy of: *The Bridgeman Art
Library:* Abraham Lincoln (1809–65) 1864 (coloured engraving) American School (19th century) Private
Collection. Peter Newark American Pictures; *Alamy:* Popperfoto, 6, 99; The Print Collection, 52; *The
Granger Collection:* 8, 15, 17, 19, 20, 24, 17, 29, 32, 35, 37, 43, 44, 67, 80, 81, 87, 97; *NorthWind Pictures:*
10, 13; *Art Archive:* National Archives, 70; Culver, 91; *Getty Images:* Hulton Archives, 11, 22; Library of
Congress, 73; *Corbis:* Bettmann, 12, 38, 47, 55, 58, 68, 93; CORBIS, 46, 60, 64, 89; Matthew Brady, 77;
Medford Society Collection, 83; *Art Resource:* National Portrait Gallery, Smithsonian Institution, 41;
Adoc photos, 48; *The Image Works:* Heliograph, Corpus Imaginum, Hanfstaengt Collection. c Blanc
Kunstverlag/sv-Bilderdienst, 54.

Printed in Malaysia
1 3 5 6 4 2

CONTENTS

One of America's most honored heroes, Abraham Lincoln was born in a small log cabin.

ABRAHAM LINCOLN
1809 1865

Lincoln's boyhood log cabin home

From the Woods to Washington

One

On the evening of April 14, 1865, the president of the United States lay unconscious. His lanky body was too long for the bed to which he had been rushed, so he was laid out diagonally. Over the course of the evening the room filled with national leaders who grieved.

As word spread that the president had been shot, grief overtook the nation. Some of those who grieved hadn't liked the president until recently. During most of his presidency he had been widely despised. But over the past weeks his popularity had increased sharply. Now, as he lay dying, it soared.

Today, Abraham Lincoln is considered to have been one of America's greatest presidents. The years of his presidency, 1861 through 1865, dominated by a bloody civil war, were among the nation's most traumatic. But through it all Lincoln managed to keep the nation together, to oversee the outlawing of slavery, to establish once and for all that the states were permanently "united," and to prove to the world that a nation devoted to freedom could last. For this last reason it is not only Americans who are in awe of what he achieved. Around the world Lincoln is considered one of the greatest people who ever lived.

Nowhere

It's no exaggeration to say that Abraham Lincoln came from nowhere. He was born in a log cabin in the woods, miles from the

7

Thomas Lincoln was a farmer and carpenter.

nearest town, in Hardin County, Kentucky, on February 12, 1809. His father, Thomas Lincoln, had never gone to school. While working as a farmhand on the frontier, Thomas Lincoln picked up enough woodworking skills to become a carpenter. At age twenty-eight he married Nancy Hanks of Virginia, about whom little is known except that her family was described as "undistinguished." Together they had a daughter they named Sarah, and then, two years later, a son they named Abraham.

From a young age the Lincoln children were needed on the farm to help plant corn, pumpkins, and other crops. There was a schoolhouse some 2 miles from the Lincoln's cabin where the basics of reading and writing were taught. But as work on the farm always came first, Abraham attended only about one year of school over the course of his entire childhood.

After a few years building up the farm, Thomas Lincoln found that, due to confusion about property rights, someone else owned his land. So in December 1816 the Lincoln family moved to the newly formed state of Indiana.

The Lincolns' journey to Indiana was grueling. They traveled about 90 miles in five days, on horseback, on a raft, and on foot. At times they had to make their way through forests so thick with branches that "a man could scarcely get through on foot," a boyhood friend would later recall.

Indiana

Arriving at their new property in the late fall, the family needed shelter at once. So Thomas Lincoln built an emergency structure called a **half-faced camp**. Though this small, three-sided log structure was missing a fourth wall and a floor, there was a fire burning day and night on the fourth side that kept the family warm. With this temporary shelter in place, the Lincolns could begin the months-long task of building a proper log cabin. When the Lincolns' new home was complete, it contained only some three-legged stools, a table comprised of a few logs nailed together, and a loft bed made of wooden poles with a mattress of leaves. It was primitive. But compared to the half-faced camp, it was spacious and comfortable.

After building the cabin, the Lincolns had to get busy chopping down trees and clearing away bushes to turn the forest into farmland. Though only eight years old, Abraham was a great help in this effort. He was tall, or "large of his age," as he would later put it. And he was skilled with an ax, "that most useful instrument," which he could use not only to chop wood but also for protection; the wilderness was inhabited by bears, wolves, and panthers.

Though skilled at clearing land and farming, young Abraham wasn't comfortable with every aspect of frontier life. One day he stuck his rifle through an opening in the cabin wall to blast a turkey at close range and learned that hunting was not for him. He would later write that after that incident he had "never since pulled trigger on any larger game." The sensitive boy had a hatred of bloodshed that would last throughout his life.

Growing up on the frontier, Lincoln became skilled with an ax.

Abraham's sensitivity was tested far more deeply at age nine, when his mother died of "milk sickness," probably caused by drinking milk from a cow that had eaten a poisonous root. In the frontier tradition Nancy Lincoln was given no formal funeral or cemetery burial when she died; Thomas Lincoln buried his wife on a hill near the log cabin. Shortly after losing their mother, Abraham and Sarah also had to do without their father, who returned to Kentucky to find a new wife. A few months later Thomas was back with his new bride, Sarah Bush Johnston, and her three children from a prior marriage.

Lincoln's stepmother Sarah remembered him as "the best boy I ever saw."

Through all these changes Abraham kept growing faster than his peers. By age fifteen he was 6 feet tall. His long legs and strong arms suited him well for the rugged environment. But it was his mental skills that set him apart. Lacking formal schooling, Abraham educated himself. Though paper and writing utensils were rare on the frontier, Abraham found other ways to practice math and writing. As his stepmother would later recall, Abraham would write "on boards when he had no paper or no slate and when the board would get too black he would shave it off with a drawing knife and go on again."

Above all, the boy loved books, and would walk for miles to get a hold of them. Two of Abraham's favorite books were Aesop's fables and the Bible, which he read over and over. As an adult he would quote from both works in speeches. He also loved a popular biography of George Washington. While reading about

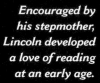

Encouraged by his stepmother, Lincoln developed a love of reading at an early age.

Washington's historic crossing of the Delaware River, Abraham sensed that "there must have been something more than common that those men struggled for," he would later recall. As an adult he would come up with his own answer for what that "something more" was.

By age twenty Abraham was a gangly 6 foot 4 inches with big hands and feet, long arms, big ears sticking out, coarse hair sticking up, and a face that was often described as "homely." But if he didn't impress people with his looks, he could win them with his charm, using his high voice to do imitations and tell jokes

As a young man Lincoln got a job taking cargo down the Ohio River on a flatboat.

and stories. The lanky young man was able to earn money as a hired hand, since he was skilled at cutting wood, plowing fields, cutting corn, threshing wheat, and splitting rails to build cabins and fences. Eventually, Abraham was given a job floating a flatboat to the bustling seaport of New Orleans, Louisiana. This job gave him a chance to see the world beyond Indiana, and it whetted his appetite for travel and independence. At twenty-one, Abraham Lincoln was ready to leave home.

New Salem

Over the coming months Lincoln's wanderings led him to New Salem, Illinois, where he took a job as a clerk in a general store. New Salem was a village comprised of log cabins, a mill, a saloon, and a few stores. But compared to the woods in which Lincoln had been raised, it was a big city. There were even a few intellectuals among the settlers. A village philosopher introduced him to the work of great poets such as William Shakespeare, whose plays Lincoln came to treasure.

There were hardly enough people in New Salem to buy the products Lincoln sold in the store. But this worked to the young man's advantage. With plenty of time on his hands, Lincoln would spend hours a day sitting in the store and reading. He would also use his free time to visit the local court, where he enjoyed hearing legal arguments. He took part in some debates in a local debate club, too. He even tried his hand at wrestling, taking part in a match to entertain his friends.

Lincoln made a good impression on the people of New Salem, who respected him for his brains and his strength. Above all, he had a reputation for honesty, which he earned with his passionate devotion to repaying debts. When the general store failed and Lincoln was left jobless, a neighbor noted that "Lincoln's got nothing, only friends."

Lincoln's unemployment didn't last long though, because of the Black Hawk War. The Black Hawk tribe had been moved from Illinois to Iowa by the U. S. government as the result of a disputed treaty. When Chief Black Hawk led a band of warriors to try to reclaim the land they believed was theirs, the governor of Illinois called volunteers to stop them. Lincoln volunteered and was

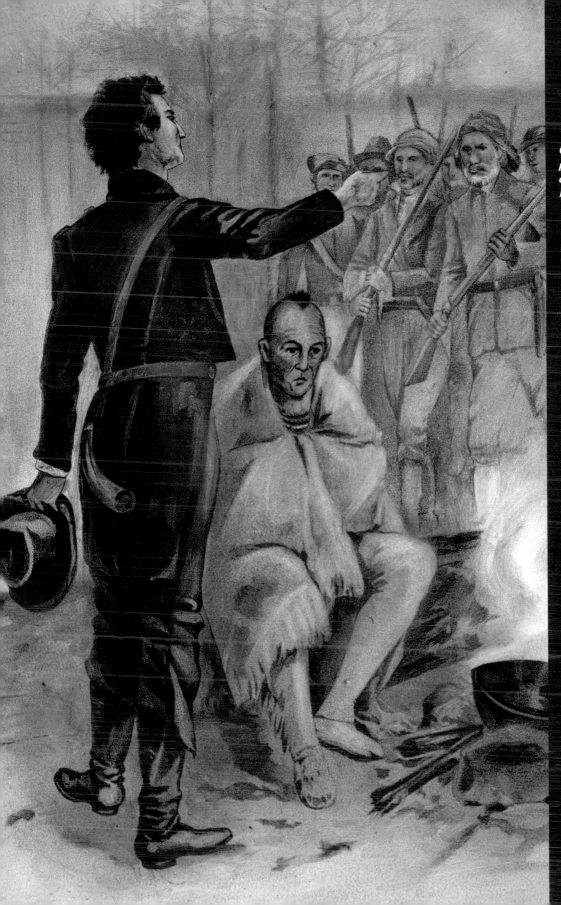

Captain Lincoln
protects a prisoner
during the Black
Hawk War.

elected captain by the men of his company. Though Lincoln never saw any fighting in the Black Hawk War, he got a taste of leadership, and liked it.

After the war Lincoln took his first step into politics, running for the **state legislature** in the election of 1832. Though he was defeated, he received 277 of the 300 votes cast in his district. Clearly, people who knew this young man loved him. In 1834 Lincoln made sure more people knew him and loved him by traveling around the county shaking hands. And it worked; he was elected to the state legislature.

Before this second campaign, Lincoln had joined a new political party called the **Whigs**. Formed to oppose President Andrew Jackson and his Democrats, the Whigs wanted government to play a bigger role in helping the country grow. Lincoln went on to become a leader of the Whigs in the Illinois state legislature, as he was elected to serve three more terms. Over these years he argued in favor of a central bank of Illinois, and he supported efforts to build railroads and canals through the state.

Shortly after being elected to the legislature, Lincoln decided to do something most of his peers in the legislature had already done: study law. There were only seven law schools in the country in those days. So Lincoln studied law on his own, sometimes walking 20 miles to the big city of Springfield for books. "He read so much," a friend remembered, "that he became emaciated and his best friends were afraid that he would craze himself."

SPRINGFIELD

In 1837, after passing the bar exam, Lincoln moved to Springfield to begin his law career. Lawyers of Lincoln's day were often

Ha to the Chief

"Our greatest president was also our funniest president," claims former senator Bob Dole in his book *Great Presidential Wit*. Like Dole, most historians rate Lincoln first among presidents when it comes to wit. By combining frontier frankness with a sharp intellect, Lincoln was able to generate humorous stories and witty remarks that could keep friends and political foes alike howling with laughter.

Often Lincoln used his wit to make fun of himself. For example, when Illinois senator Stephen Douglas accused Lincoln of being two-faced, Lincoln replied, "If I had another face, do you think I would wear this one?" When other politicians bragged about their bold military feats, Lincoln would mock his own Black Hawk War achievements, saying, "I had a good many bloody battles with the mosquitoes!"

During his presidency, among the most common victims of Lincoln's wit were his generals, most of whom he found ineffective. Hearing that the enemy had captured one of his generals and twelve army mules, Lincoln remarked, "How unfortunate. Those mules cost us two hundred dollars a piece." Against supporters of slavery Lincoln aimed this memorable mock: "Whenever I hear anyone arguing for slavery, I feel a strong impulse to see it tried on him personally."

(continued)

Many of Lincoln's witty remarks were simple observations about the ironies of life. For example, during a period in which Lincoln was especially weary of people begging him for jobs, the White House doctor found that Lincoln was suffering from a mild form of smallpox. "Is it contagious?" asked Lincoln. "Very contagious," his doctor replied, causing Lincoln to smile. When the doctor asked why this news pleased Lincoln, the president replied, "Now I have something I can give everybody."

In spite of all his joking, Lincoln found his presidency to be a time of nearly constant stress and suffering. "I laugh because if I didn't I would weep," he confessed.

stereotyped as being tricky or greedy. But "honest Abe" Lincoln became known as a different sort of lawyer. He encouraged people to settle out of court, even when doing so would cost him his fee. As he explained in a letter to a friend, "As a peace-maker the lawyer has a superior opportunity of being a good man. There will still be business enough." When cases did go to trial Lincoln got a chance to hone his speaking skills, explaining complex matters to uneducated juries in such a way that people understood completely.

Though articulate and confident as a lawyer, Lincoln was awkward and uncomfortable with women. The first woman he asked to marry him rejected him, leaving Lincoln convinced he'd never find a wife. But hope was reborn when he was attending a party at a friend's house and met the lively socialite Mary Todd.

Lincoln and Mary were opposites in many ways. He was tall and thin, she was short and stout. He was easygoing and sloppy, she was high-strung and stylish. While he had been raised in poverty, she came from a wealthy, well-known family. But in spite of their differences, they shared a love of poetry and politics. Soon they decided to share their lives as well. In November 1842, when Lincoln was thirty-three and Mary Todd twenty-three, they married.

In 1842 Lincoln married the smart and stylish Mary Todd.

In the first four years of their marriage the couple had two sons, Robert and Edward. Then, in 1846, Lincoln decided to make an ambitious career move. After serving for nearly a decade in state government, he set his sights on national office: he would run as the Whig candidate for his district's seat in the U.S. Congress.

Lincoln's campaign for Congress was going smoothly until his opponent, a minister named Peter Cartwright, attacked him, claiming that Lincoln was against religion. The charge was not without basis. While most settlers on the frontier were formally attached to one church or another, Lincoln never declared a denominational affiliation.

Lincoln responded to Cartwright's charge with a pamphlet in which he stated that he would never belittle any man's faith, while managing to remain vague about his own. He admitted to having

*Congressman
Abraham
Lincoln*

privately considered that a "Doctrine of Necessity" controls human life. According to this theory, which is more akin to philosophy or science than religion, people's actions are controlled by forces over which they have no control. In future speeches, Lincoln often made a point of referring to God. But the God Lincoln described tended to sound mysterious and unpredictable, like an inevitable force of nature.

If there was an inevitable force in Lincoln's life, it was moving him toward power. Impressed by his honest response to Cartwright, voters elected Lincoln to represent them in Washington. Meanwhile, the country Lincoln had chosen to serve was moving toward an inevitable crisis.

Where slavery was legal, human beings were bought and sold like cattle.

THE GREAT DEBATE Two

$\mathcal{T}$he first European settlers who came to America lived with a contradiction. They believed deeply and passionately in their right to be free. But many of them also believed in their right to keep Africans as slaves. When it was time to establish a nation, the founding fathers tried to resolve this contradiction. Some felt slavery should be illegal in the new nation. Others felt the right to own slaves should be guaranteed. Unable to agree, the founding fathers decided to put off resolving the issue in the hopes that it would go away. But it didn't go away. As the country grew, disagreement about slavery intensified.

ANTISLAVERY LINCOLN

Abraham Lincoln was opposed to slavery. He saw few slaves when he was growing up, since slavery was illegal in Indiana. But on a boat trip to Kentucky in 1847–1848 Lincoln saw a dozen slaves chained together like animals, and it troubled him deeply. "That sight was continual torment to me," Lincoln would later write.

To justify his belief that slavery didn't belong in America, Lincoln turned to the Declaration of Independence and its assertion that all men are created equal. "The relation of masters and slaves," Lincoln insisted, "is a total violation of this principle." Lincoln felt that the declaration's principle of equality would gradually be applied to people of every race, across the country and around the world.

Lincoln was not an **abolitionist**. He did not believe that Congress had the right to interfere with slavery where it

HUMAN PROPERTY

When Abraham Lincoln became president, the crisis over slavery was reaching a new intensity. But slavery itself was not new. Since the dawn of recorded time, some human beings have owned others.

In the earliest human societies people captured during a war were commonly enslaved by their captors and made to work in their fields. Thieves and people who couldn't pay their debts might also be forced to become slaves. Throughout the ancient world—from Egypt and Mesopotamia (now Iraq) to China and India—slavery was common, as it was in some tribal societies of Africa and the Americas. Slavery was especially widespread in the empires of Greece and Rome, where slaves did most of the work.

During the Middle Ages slavery was less common. But in the 1400s a new need for human labor arose, as European exploration led to the

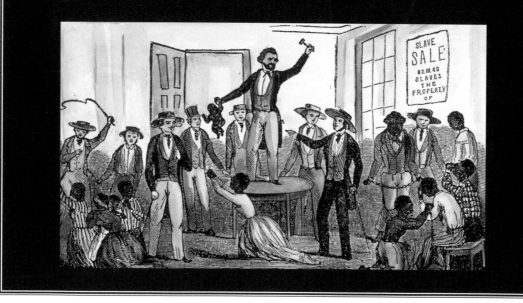

establishment of colonies in Africa and North and South America. To work in the mines and fields of these colonies, Europeans enslaved the natives, or brought slaves from other lands. Between the 1500s and the early 1800s, over twelve million people were brought from Africa to the Americas to work as slaves. During this period slavery came to be closely linked to race. European masters convinced themselves that their African slaves deserved to be enslaved because white people were somehow better than black people.

In the United States at the time of Lincoln's election to Congress, almost all the nation's slaves were in the South, where they worked mainly on cotton and tobacco plantations. Nearly one in three people living in the South at this time was a slave. With no legal rights, the slaves were often mistreated. Most were forced to spend every waking hour working in the fields before being crammed into filthy huts at night. For punishment they might be whipped, beaten, or kept in chains. Slaves were not allowed to vote, marry, or learn to read or write. Because slaves were sold at the will of their owners, parents and children were often separated.

In ancient times, few questioned whether slavery was fair; it was accepted as a fact of life. But during the 1700s philosophers and religious leaders began to embrace the idea that all people were entitled to certain human rights, such as the right to be free. Though the founders of the United States believed in these human rights in general, some of the founders worried the southern economy would collapse without slaves, so slavery continued. In 1833 the British government abolished all slavery. In 1848 French slaves were freed as well. But in the southern United States slavery continued to thrive until the age-old practice was stopped by a civil war.

already existed. Instead, Lincoln predicted that over time slavery would die a natural death, as it was doing in England and France.

By today's standards, some of the views Lincoln expressed are racist. While addressing a proslavery crowd he granted that there might be significant differences between blacks and whites. During his presidency Lincoln briefly considered "colonization," a plan by which freed slaves would be encouraged to form their own country in Africa. Though this was only one of many solutions he considered for dealing with freed slaves, in retrospect it is as racist as it is ridiculous. But throughout his career Lincoln was clear and consistent in his belief that people of all races deserved to be free. "If slavery is not wrong, nothing is wrong," he proclaimed.

While serving in the Illinois state legislature Lincoln had occasion to make his antislavery views known; when the legislature voted to condemn abolition societies, Lincoln and one other representative filed a protest. In the U.S. **House of Representatives** he would have a chance to make a difference about slavery on a much greater scale.

IN THE HOUSE

When Lincoln entered Congress in December 1847, the United States was at war with Mexico for control of Texas and other southwestern territory. The Mexican War was linked to the slavery debate. Antislavery advocates worried that adding southern territory to the United States would mean more states where slavery was allowed.

Like many Whigs, Lincoln opposed the Mexican War, and as a congressman, he gave voice to his opposition. In a fiery

In the Mexican War, the United States battled with Mexico for control of Texas and other South-western territory.

speech on the floor of the House of Representatives, Lincoln suggested that President James K. Polk had lied when claiming that the war was begun by Mexicans killing Americans on American soil. At the climax of his speech, Lincoln challenged the president to show the exact spot of American soil on which American blood had been spilt. For this reason, the speech became known as the Spot Resolutions.

Criticizing the president so severely in time of war was considered unpatriotic by many Americans. A group of citizens in Lincoln's own state announced that never before had such "black odium and infamy" been heaped on "the living brave and illustrious dead." An Illinois newspaper taunted that Lincoln had a disease called spotted fever, which would mean political doom for "Spotty Lincoln." Unmoved by Lincoln's bold words, Congress continued to support the president, and the war.

Aside from the Spot Resolutions, Lincoln's term in Congress was uneventful. He supported Whig plans to increase government spending on roads and other public improvements. He supported taxes on foreign goods, in keeping with the Whig plan to protect the nation's businesses. And after the United States won the Mexican War, he supported the Wilmot Proviso, which was intended to keep slavery out of the newly acquired southwestern territory.

As his term drew to a close, Lincoln was anxious to stay in Congress. "If it should so happen that nobody else wishes to be elected," he hinted, "I could not refuse the people the right of sending me." But the people didn't clamor to send him back. So after only two years in Washington, Lincoln returned to his law practice in Springfield.

But tragedy awaited the Lincolns in Illinois, as their three-year-old son, Edward, died of tuberculosis in February 1850. Ten months after the loss of Edward, a new Lincoln, William ("Willie"), was born. And in 1853 another boy, Thomas, was added to the family. As an infant, Thomas had a large head, which made him look somewhat like a tadpole and earned this last of the Lincoln children the nickname "Tad."

The Kansas-Nebraska Act

In 1854 Lincoln was drawn back into politics when Congress passed the controversial Kansas-Nebraska Act. The Missouri Compromise of 1820 had outlawed slavery in territories north of Missouri's southern border, except for Missouri itself. But now Illinois senator Stephen Douglas was proposing that settlers who moved into the northern territories of Kansas and Nebraska should be allowed to have slaves if they so desired. As Lincoln saw it, by limiting the extension of slavery, the Missouri Compromise put slavery on the path to ultimate extinction; but the Kansas-Nebraska Act was a big step backward.

As Douglas came around the state to speak in favor of the Kansas-Nebraska Act, Lincoln followed him around speaking against it. While opposing Douglas, Lincoln began drifting back into national politics. He supported an anti-Douglas candidate for Congress, but the candidate was defeated. Then he ran for Senate himself. On the first ballot Lincoln had almost enough votes to win. On successive ballots his votes dwindled. Finally, Lincoln withdrew his name and supported another candidate to prevent a Douglas supporter from being elected.

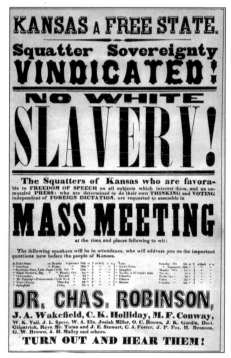

This 1854 poster announces a meeting for anti-slavery settlers who opposed the Kansas-Nebraska Act.

As the country was becoming increasingly divided over the slavery issue, so was the Whig Party. Northern and southern Whigs disagreed so strongly about slavery that the party had to disband. In its wake another party came together that appealed to northern Whigs such as Lincoln. Formed in 1854, the Republican Party was opposed to the expansion of slavery. Lincoln joined in 1856 and quickly became one of its most vocal figures. Later that year, when the party nominated California governor John Frémont as its first presidential candidate, Lincoln received a number of votes to be the Republican candidate for vice president.

Though the Republicans lost the election, they were encouraged by their strong second-place finish, but they had little time for celebration. A few months later, the **Supreme Court** announced its controversial *Dred Scott* decision. According to this decision, slaves were considered property; they had no rights and they could never be free in any state. Lincoln felt the *Dred Scott* decision did "obvious violence" to the Declaration of Independence.

THE GREAT DEBATES

In 1858 Lincoln was again nominated for the Senate, this time to run against Stephen Douglas. In accepting the nomination Lincoln gave his most provocative speech yet, in which he insisted:

A house divided against itself cannot stand. I believe this nation cannot endure permanently half slave and half free. I do not expect the Union to be dissolved—I do not expect the house to fall—But I do expect it will cease to be divided. It will become all one thing or all the other.

A stable house was something Lincoln appreciated. He had built log cabins with his own hands. He understood the painstaking care required for their construction. And he knew how vital it was that a house stand strong, so its residents would be safe from harsh weather and wild animals. But while comparing the United States to a house in danger of falling, Lincoln's speech gave the house a violent shake. A "house divided" was what many southerners wanted so that supporters and opponents of slavery could live together in peace. By claiming that this division was unacceptable, Lincoln turned up the heat on the national conflict.

Then Lincoln challenged his Democratic opponent to a series of debates. Though Douglas was favored to win reelection, the senator accepted Lincoln's challenge. Over the next two months the two men met in seven debates held in towns across the state.

Though both Lincoln and Douglas were skilled debaters, in other ways they were striking opposites. While the tall, thin Lincoln spoke in a high voice, the short, squat Douglas was a baritone. Their differences of opinion were just as striking. In each debate Douglas argued that slavery should be left up to the people. But Lincoln insisted that slavery was unjust, and that it had no place in a democracy—a government set up to serve the common people. "It is the eternal struggle between two principles—right and wrong," Lincoln said of his conflict with Douglas. "The one is the common right of humanity, the other the divine right of kings."

Wherever the debaters went, huge crowds gathered to watch them battle. According to the debate format, each debater

During the 1858 senate race, Lincoln and Stephen Douglas confronted each other in a series of debates.

ILLINOIS BORN UNDER THE ORDINANCE OF '87.

"WESTWARD THE STAR OF E
THE GIRLS LINK ON TO L
THEIR MOTHERS

ABE
THE
GIANT-KILLER

was allowed to speak for over an hour at a time. But the listeners stood with rapt attention, cheering their favorite candidate when he made an impressive point and demanding more when the debate was finished. Reporters from national newspapers attended the debates as well, putting the contest on the national stage. By the last debate, Douglas's deep voice had become so hoarse from shouting that it was hard to understand. Lincoln's high voice still carried over the crowd.

On election day Lincoln barely lost and Douglas was reelected to the Senate. But Lincoln's performance in the debates had made him a national leader of the fight to contain slavery. When invited to speak at Cooper Union in New York City, Lincoln realized this was the perfect chance for the Republican from the west to make his views known in the east. After careful preparation, he delivered a detailed argument in which he attempted to prove that the founding fathers had believed that slavery would someday be outlawed. The speech ended with a rallying cry to Republicans that Lincoln wrote entirely in capital letters:

LET US HAVE FAITH THAT RIGHT MAKES MIGHT, AND IN THAT FAITH, LET US, TO THE END, DARE TO DO OUR DUTY AS WE UNDERSTAND IT.

Though defeated in the senatorial election, Abraham Lincoln had just begun to fight.

RUNNING FOR PRESIDENT

At the Republican Convention of 1860 the delegates had trouble finding a candidate for president on whom they could agree.

Though Senator William Seward of New York had the most delegates, he also had many enemies within the party. Another leading Republican, Governor Salmon Chase of Ohio, couldn't even unite the delegates from his own state.

Because Lincoln was seen as a moderate on the slavery question and was well liked throughout the party, Republicans began to look to Lincoln to bring the party together. On the third ballot, Lincoln won his party's nomination for president. To balance the ticket geographically and politically, a former Democrat from Maine named Hannibal Hamlin was chosen as the candidate for vice president.

Though Lincoln had only two years of experience serving in the federal government, Republicans found a way to turn their candidate's lack of experience into a plus. Drawing on the fact that Lincoln had at one time earned a living splitting rails, Republicans portrayed Lincoln as "the Rail Splitter candidate of 1860." In slogans, songs, and paintings they emphasized the former rail splitter's physical strength and humble background.

When the Democrats met to choose their candidate, southern and northern wings of the party were unable to agree—so they separated. Northern Democrats, who believed the people of a state should be able to decide whether slavery is legal in that state, chose Stephen Douglas as their candidate. Southern Democrats, who believed slavery should be allowed anywhere, chose John Breckinridge of Kentucky.

As if three candidates were not enough, the election of 1860 featured the formation of yet another party: the Constitutional Union Party. Dedicated to preserving the Union at all costs, members of this fourth party chose John Bell of Tennessee as their candidate.

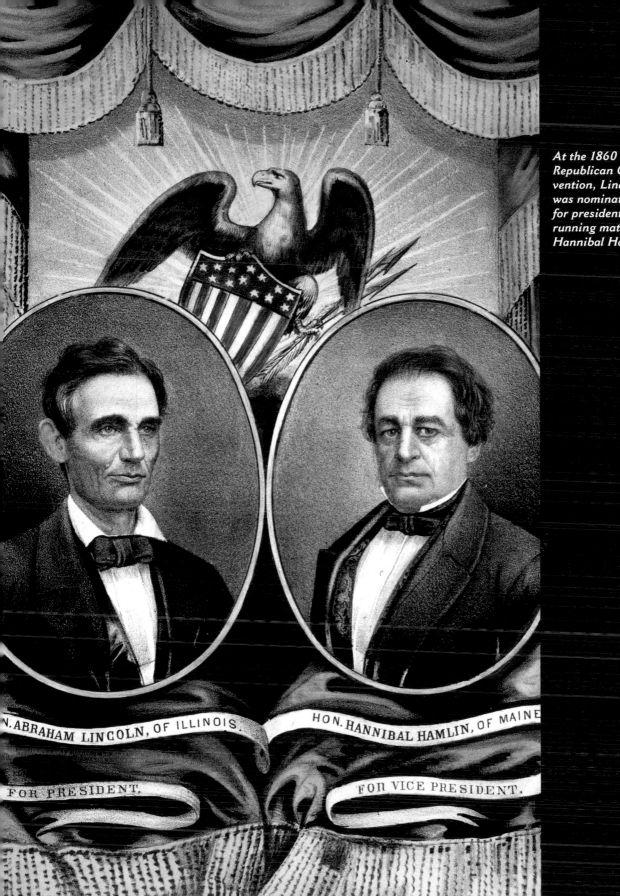

N. ABRAHAM LINCOLN, OF ILLINOIS.

HON. HANNIBAL HAMLIN, OF MAINE

FOR PRESIDENT.

FOR VICE PRESIDENT.

With the fate of slavery and the preservation of the Union itself at stake, supporters of all four candidates campaigned vigorously. The race quickly broke down into two separate battles: Lincoln versus Douglas in the north and Breckinridge versus Bell in the south. Bell supporters rang bells of every shape and size to inspire patriotism and win votes. Breckinridge supporters scared voters by warning that a Republican victory would mean the loss of their slaves. President Buchanan and two former presidents, John Tyler and Franklin Pierce, urged people to vote for Breckinridge; in their view, the southern Democrat was the only candidate who could keep the south from leaving the Union. Douglas campaigned all across the north, urging voters to elect a statesman and not a rail splitter. He campaigned in the south, too, where he urged citizens to accept the result, whatever it might be.

But it was the Republicans who campaigned most effectively. They held parades of torchbearing marchers called wide awakes. They held parades that featured battalions of marching rail splitters. They even held parades in which all the marchers were exactly as tall as their candidate—whose height of 6 feet 4 inches was remarkable in comparison to the average height of the day.

Through all the excitement Lincoln stayed in Springfield and avoided making campaign speeches. But he did make one move to help his chances, in response to an unusual letter from an eleven-year-old girl named Grace Bedell. " [I]f you will let your whiskers grow . . . you would look a great deal better for your face is so thin," the child wrote, urging Lincoln to grow a beard. "All the ladies like whiskers and they would tease their husbands to vote for you and then you would be President." There had

This political cartoon from 1860 captures the raucous spirit of the battle between Douglas and Lincoln for the presidency.

never been a bearded president before. But Lincoln was willing to take the risk.

Whether the beard affected the outcome or not, the nation's divided political climate certainly did. On election day Lincoln only won 39 percent of the popular vote, significantly less than half, but far more than any of the other candidates received. So, even though 60 percent of the voters had voted for his opponents, Abraham Lincoln would be the next president of the United States.

This photo is one of the last taken before Lincoln grew a beard at the request of eleven-year-old Grace Bedell.

Though Republicans had chosen Lincoln because he was a moderate, southerners—recalling his "house divided" speech—feared that Lincoln posed a threat to their right to own slaves and to the southern economy. And they believed that if the Union was no longer serving their interests, they had a right to leave it.

On December 20, 1860, South Carolina announced that it was seceding, or leaving the Union. President Buchanan felt he could do nothing in response. And as he continued to do nothing, six other southern states followed South Carolina's lead. The house Lincoln had been elected to watch over was collapsing.

STRAINED BY PASSION

*O*n February 11, 1861, before leaving Springfield to head to Washington, D.C., Lincoln gave an emotional farewell speech to his friends and neighbors. "I now leave, not knowing when, or whether ever, I may return," he said, "with a task before me greater than that which rested upon Washington." In saying his task was more difficult than George Washington's, Lincoln wasn't exaggerating. While the first president had been called to unite the eager citizens of the young nation, Lincoln would have to unite angry citizens—many of whom didn't want to be part of the nation at all.

UNITY AT ALL COSTS

Most Southerners felt secession was justified if it was in their best interest, because the United States had been set up to serve the interests of the people. But Lincoln disagreed. If the people in a democracy didn't like the leader, they could elect a new one, but they couldn't just leave. If states left every time they didn't like the results of an election, Lincoln reasoned, government controlled by the people would die out, and people would go back to being ruled by kings and dictators. As much as Lincoln hated slavery, he felt preserving the Union was even more urgent, since he believed that if the states stayed united, slavery would eventually die out. For the sake of freedom in the south and around the world, Lincoln believed the Union had to be preserved.

Lincoln's cabinet included his former rivals William Seward, who is seated closest to Lincoln, and Salmon Chase, who is standing closest to Lincoln.

In addition to unifying the nation, Lincoln had to unify his party. Shortly after being elected, Lincoln chose a cabinet that included men who represented a range of viewpoints within the Republican Party. He chose William H. Seward and Salmon P. Chase, leading Republicans who had been his main rivals for the presidential nomination, as his secretary of state and secretary of treasury.

On his way toward Washington, Lincoln toured the North to get Northerners solidly behind him. But while solidifying his support in the North, he was careful to avoid provoking Southerners. When asked what he would do about the states that had left the Union, Lincoln's response was always calm, vague, and noncommittal. "I must run the machine as I find it," he said.

But Lincoln's attempts at keeping people calm didn't stop **secessionists** from moving ahead with their plans. On February 18, 1861, they formed the **Confederate States of America**, with a constitution based on the U.S. Constitution—except that it declared slavery legal. Then they elected Mississippi senator Jefferson Davis as their president.

Even in the North, Lincoln was not safe from secessionists' hatred. In Philadelphia, Lincoln was informed of a plot against his life. So he cut short his trip and covertly boarded an overnight train to Washington, where he arrived in secret the next morning. Typically, a president-elect arrives in the nation's capital like a victorious hero and does not have to sneak into town. But these were not typical times.

On March 4, 1861, Lincoln took the oath of office, as all presidents before him had, vowing to "preserve, protect, and defend the Constitution." Then he faced the crowd to present his much awaited **inaugural address**. In it, Lincoln implored angry Southerners to forget about leaving the Union. He declared that he would not interfere with slavery where it already existed. He appealed to the history they had shared with Northerners.

But Lincoln also made it clear that he would defend the Constitution, which he believed did not allow states to secede. "In *your* hands, my dissatisfied fellow-countrymen, and not mine, is the momentous issue of civil war," he asserted. "*You* have no oath registered in Heaven to destroy the government, while I shall have the most solemn one to 'preserve, protect,

The seceding states elected Jefferson Davis of Mississippi president of the Confederate States.

WORKAHOLIC PRESIDENT

For all its challenges, the job of president has one distinct advantage: you get to choose your own hours. Some presidents have felt they served most effectively by keeping a leisurely schedule, arriving at their White House office in the late morning, departing in the late afternoon, and taking regular extended vacations.

At the other end of the spectrum was Abraham Lincoln, one of the hardest working presidents of all. Lincoln commonly headed to the office at the crack of dawn and stayed late into the evening. Mary Lincoln considered herself lucky if her husband made it back to their living quarters by eleven at night.

One thing that kept Lincoln busy was his meetings with countless members of the public. Other presidents had been besieged by citizens asking favors or just wanting to meet the president. But Lincoln devoted more time to chatting with these visitors than any of his predecessors had. In the days before polling, Lincoln found these "public opinion baths," as he called them, a useful way to get a sense of how the people felt.

Lincoln's schedule was also filled with tasks relating to the war, such as visits to military hospitals and army camps, and visits to the telegraph office for the latest news on how a battle was progressing. Owing largely to the relentless burdens of the war, Lincoln spent less than one month away from the White House during his entire presidency.

and defend' it." In closing, Lincoln's words became emotional and even poetic. "We are not enemies, but friends. We must not be enemies," he said. "Though passion may have strained, it must not break our bonds of affection."

WAR BEGINS

But for many Southerners, the "bonds of affection" Lincoln had invoked were already broken. In South Carolina, rebels surrounded Fort Sumter in Charleston Harbor and ordered the federal troops inside to surrender. Lincoln was afraid to send reinforcements to the fort, since that would seem to be provoking war. But he also didn't want to allow the Union troops to withdraw, since that would seem cowardly. So he took a middle road and simply had the fort resupplied with rations so the soldiers could hold out longer. The standoff ended in the early morning of

On April 12, 1861, Confederate troops fired on Fort Sumter, beginning the Civil War.

April 12 when Confederates opened fire on the fort. After exchanging fire with the Confederates for a day, the Union soldiers surrendered. The American Civil War had begun.

In pursuing the war, Lincoln never described the South as a foreign country. He was careful to avoid even acknowledging that the Confederacy existed. He spoke of the conflict not as a war but as an illegal rebellion that needed to be stopped.

Describing the conflict this way gave Lincoln an advantage. When the United States is going to war, the president isn't supposed to command the army to fight until **Congress** officially declares war. But during a national emergency the president can command the army to act without waiting for Congress to approve. Since Lincoln defined the Southerners who were taking up arms as rebels rather than citizens of a foreign country, he could use the army to oppose them. Without waiting for Congressional approval, Lincoln called up 75,000 volunteers to serve a three-month term of military duty, beginning immediately. He also ordered the navy to blockade Southern ports, so Southerners couldn't sell their cotton overseas.

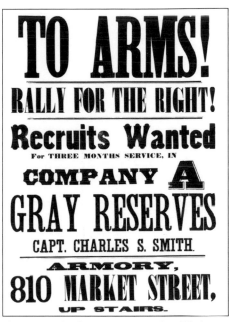

An army draft notice, posted in Philadelphia, calls men to arms to serve in the Civil War.

Lincoln insisted that he was taking these steps in response to Southern aggression. But people throughout the South were offended that the president would raise an army to take arms against states. So four more southern states seceded, including Virginia. Besides being the largest, Virginia was the closest southern state to the nation's capital. Now Lincoln could see Confederate flags flying in Arlington, Virginia from his White House window.

The Union Struggles

The first meeting of the armies took place on July 21, 1861, in Manassas, Virginia, in a battle named the Battle of Bull Run after a nearby stream. Expecting the war to be brief, civilians came carrying picnic baskets to watch the fighting as they might a sporting event. But what they witnessed was no game. After a day of bloody battle, Union troops were driven back in an embarrassing defeat that convinced people on both sides that this war would not be brief.

To pay for the war, Lincoln made the unpopular move of proposing new taxes. Also unpopular was his decision to extend the term of enlistment in the army from three months to two years. A third move Lincoln needed to make at this time was to find a general to lead the army. Lincoln's original choice was the man with the best reputation in the military, Robert E. Lee. But Lee was true to his home state of Virginia, so when Virginia seceded he joined the Confederate army. So did most other Southern officers.

Lincoln appointed Major General George McClellan to lead the Union troops.

Eventually, Lincoln settled on Major General George McClellan, whose skill at training volunteers would prove valuable. McClellan was a handsome man who had a gift for public relations and was able to say the right thing to the right person to advance his career. Though McClellan knew how to talk to politicians, he had little respect for their understanding of war. He felt Lincoln was particularly ignorant about military matters. "The president is an idiot," McClellan wrote in a letter to his wife after his first meeting with Lincoln. The next time he met with Lincoln, the general sat and listened politely and then wrote to his wife, "The president is nothing more than a well-meaning baboon."

As McClellan was privately insulting Lincoln, another general was causing Lincoln grief. Frémont, the former Republican candidate for president, was now a Union general leading the fight against rebels in Missouri. Frustrated in his struggle to crush the rebels, General Frémont declared that slaves belonging to Missouri's rebels were officially free. Lincoln, determined to stick with his promise not to interfere with slavery where it already existed, ordered Frémont to take back his declaration. When Frémont refused, Lincoln removed the general from his post.

Some in the North were appalled that Lincoln would prevent slaves from being freed. An emerging group, known as the Radical Republicans, believed that fighting to save the Union should not be the only war aim. Why not fight to make the slaves free? But Lincoln was cautious. If the war were defined as being about ending slavery, the Northern states where slavery was still legal—Kentucky, Missouri, Maryland, and Delaware—would leave the Union. Without these four **border states**, Lincoln did not think the North had a chance of winning the war.

At this time Lincoln had to grapple with a grave threat coming from overseas. The Union navy had stopped a British ship, the *Trent*, coming from the South, and removed two Confederate diplomats. The British felt international law gave them the right to meet with representatives of the Confederacy, and they were willing to fight for that right. The French announced that they would stand by the British in this matter. Determined to fight only one war at a time, Lincoln backed down and released the Southern diplomats.

Backing down in a standoff with foreign powers made Lincoln look bad in the eyes of his citizens. But essentially everything he had done during his first year in office upset, angered, or offended someone, whether it was raising taxes, raising an army, trying to calm rebels, or standing up to them. He had been opposed by **radicals**, **conservatives**, Democrats, Republicans, slave owners, and abolitionists. His own top general was calling him an idiot. At the end of 1861 even many of Lincoln's biggest supporters questioned his ability to unite a divided nation.

THE LAST CARD

By the beginning of 1862 the war had been going on for eight months but the Union army had made little progress. Lincoln wanted McClellan to close in on the Confederate capital of Richmond, Virginia, and bring the Confederacy to its knees. He urged McClellan to get going. He prodded, hinted, and cajoled. In keeping with his belief that a general should be able to do things his own way, Lincoln tried to be patient. But his patience was running out. On January 27 Lincoln issued the President's General War Order Number 1, calling for a Union offensive on all fronts. To the president's disappointment, McClellan ignored it.

GENERAL TROUBLE

McClellan's reluctance to follow Lincoln's orders stemmed from the general's basic approach to war. Like many military men of the day, McClellan saw war as dignified and chivalrous, featuring parades and shows of strength, rather than bloodshed. As McClellan saw it, a general's role was to intimidate the enemy with displays of power, to outfox the enemy with clever strategies, to occupy cities—but not to attack the enemy's troops directly. Lincoln longed for a general willing to crush the enemy and end the war.

McClellan informed Lincoln that he had a plan for attacking Virginia, but he insisted on keeping his plan a secret, even from the president. "If I tell [Lincoln] my plans they will be in

General Ulysses S. Grant impressed Lincoln with his aggressive approach to warfare.

the *New York Herald* tomorrow morning," McClellan told a friend, revealing his utter disrespect for his superior. "He can't keep a secret. He will tell them to Tad."

When McClellan finally did begin moving toward Richmond, his progress was slow and sporadic. McClellan blamed the quality of the roads, the width of bridges, and the weather for his delays. At one point Lincoln sarcastically asked McClellan if, since the general didn't seem to be using the troops, perhaps someone else could borrow them. Privately, Lincoln complained that McClellan had a case of "the slows."

Meanwhile, in Tennessee, Union troops were having some success. Brigadier General Ulysses S. Grant managed to take Forts Henry and Donelson from the Confederates in daring raids. In April, Grant's troops forced Confederates to retreat in a battle at Pittsburgh Landing near a church called Shiloh. When Grant was blamed for the Union's 13,000 casualties in this battle, Union politicians called for Grant's removal. "I can't spare this man: he fights," Lincoln replied.

DEPRESSION

The victories at Forts Henry and Donelson gave the Lincolns cause for celebration, but their joy was cut short. Their eleven-year-old son Willie became ill with a fever and, after a three-week struggle, died. In her sorrow, Mary was given to such frantic fits of weeping that Lincoln feared she might lose her mind. Lincoln himself plunged into a depression.

The depression Lincoln suffered at this time was not his first; he had experienced severe depressions throughout his adult life. In an earlier episode a friend noted that Lincoln could hardly speak above a whisper. "I am now the most miserable man living," Lincoln wrote at that time. "If what I feel were equally distributed to the whole human family there would not be one cheerful face on the earth."

Lincoln's grief over Willie's death, combined with his frustration over the war, plunged him into periods of intense sadness. In this he was not alone; many Americans were miserable about the way the war was going. Not only was the war pitting people who had belonged to the same nation against one another, in many cases it was pitting members of the same family against one another. For example, Mary Lincoln's youngest brother, three half-brothers, and the husbands of two of her sisters were fighting for the army her husband was determined to destroy. The Civil War was tearing the nation and its families apart.

As the war dragged on it became expensive. The enormous costs of arming, feeding, and paying soldiers threatened to ruin the Union economy. Equally dangerous for the Union was the effect the war was having on the economies of Europe. As the North

LITTLE LADY/BIG WAR

When Lincoln was young, few northerners knew slavery as anything but an abstract concept, since they hardly ever saw slaves. That changed in 1851 when people across the nation got to know a group of slaves and experience their intense suffering. The uproar that followed was real, but the slaves were not. They were fictional characters in a novel by Harriet Beecher Stowe: *Uncle Tom's Cabin, Or Life Among the Lowly*.

A mother of seven living in Cincinnati, Stowe was the daughter, sister, and wife of Protestant clergymen who spoke against slavery. Her hatred of slavery developed as she saw runaway slaves being hunted down in her own neighborhood, and mistreated in Kentucky, during a brief visit to the neighboring state. But the event that made the deepest impression was her meeting with an African-American preacher whose arms had been maimed by beatings he suffered as a slave. Though Stowe had been writing short stories, this encounter inspired her to write a longer work about the evils of slavery. The resulting novel came so quickly and effortlessly that Stowe felt it was being written by God.

The main characters in *Uncle Tom's Cabin* include a noble slave called Uncle Tom who keeps his dignity while being sold from one master to another, a slave named Eliza who makes a daring escape to freedom rather than part with her baby, and a cruel plantation owner named

Simon Legree. Though melodramatic, the novel presents facts about slavery in America that few Northerners had considered. Above all, it depicts slaves as human beings who love one another, care deeply for their children, and suffer genuine pain.

The book became an instant best seller across the United States and in England, selling 300,000 copies in its first year. Northerners who read the book became enraged by the Fugitive Slave Law of 1850, which required escaped slaves to be returned to their masters. Southerners were enraged by the book's depiction of slavery, which many found exaggerated and false. Across the country, debate intensified. The novel was adapted for the stage and presented in theaters across the country and overseas, stirring up more outrage and making Stowe one of the most famous people in the world.

Perhaps the greatest tribute to the book's power came from Lincoln himself. In 1862 the president met Stowe in the White House and greeted her, "So this is the little lady who made this big war!" In the eyes of some historians, Lincoln's point was valid; by using fiction to tell the truth, Harriet Beecher Stowe woke people up and inspired them to change their country.

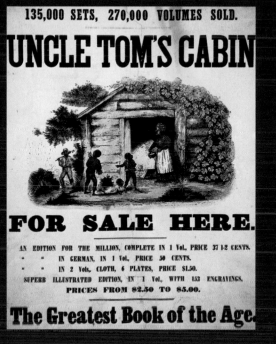

135,000 SETS, 270,000 VOLUMES SOLD.

UNCLE TOM'S CABIN

FOR SALE HERE.

AN EDITION FOR THE MILLION, COMPLETE IN 1 Vol., PRICE 37 1-2 CENTS.
" " IN GERMAN, IN 1 Vol., PRICE 50 CENTS.
" " IN 2 Vols., CLOTH, 6 PLATES, PRICE $1.50.
SUPERB ILLUSTRATED EDITION, IN 1 Vol., WITH 153 ENGRAVINGS,
PRICES FROM $2.50 TO $5.00.

The Greatest Book of the Age.

blockaded Southern ports, European mills were deprived of cotton and forced to close down. This led to massive unemployment overseas. For this reason, European nations considered joining the war on the side of the Confederacy.

A New Tactic

Toward the summer, as all was looking most bleak for the Union, Lincoln began to consider shaking things up with a bold political move: freeing slaves. "We had reached the end of our rope on the plan of operations we had been pursuing," he later wrote. "We had about played our last card and must change our tactics, or lose the game."

There were different ways in which freeing slaves could save "the game" for the Union. England and France had outlawed slavery. If the north was fighting to defeat slavery (and not just to preserve the Union), those nations would be reluctant to ally with the slaveholding south. Also, it would give a moral purpose to the war; some Northerners would be inspired to fight by this noble cause. Though Lincoln had opposed freeing slaves at the outset, as the war progressed, he could not deny that slavery had caused the war.

But not all Northerners felt that way. Many Northern conservatives would never fight to free slaves. For this reason Lincoln had to prepare the country for this change in strategy very carefully. He tried to brace conservatives for the change by writing a letter to the *New York Tribune*. In this letter he explained that, although it was his "personal wish" that all men be free, his main goal as president was to save the Union in any way he could. "If I could save the Union without freeing *any* slave I would do it," he explained, "and if I could save it by freeing *all* the slaves I would do it." Then he mentioned a third possibility, "And if I could save it by freeing some and leaving others alone I would also do that." This third option was exactly what Lincoln was planning to do.

In June, Lincoln turned his attention to writing the document in which he would announce that he was freeing some slaves. He wrote it slowly, in several sittings, while waiting at the telegraph office for news about the war. "He would look out of the window a while and then put his pen to paper," the telegraph operator noted, "but he did not write much at once. . . . He would put down a line or two and then sit quiet for a few minutes." After weeks of careful writing and revising, Lincoln was finished.

When Lincoln read the document to the members of his cabinet, **Secretary of State** Seward advised him not to issue it just yet. Freeing the slaves when the Union was faring so poorly would appear to be an act of desperation, Seward insisted. Lincoln agreed to wait for a Union victory.

But victory was a long time coming. As the Union lost one battle after another, Lincoln began to wonder if he would ever have a chance to make his announcement. McClellan's Virginia campaign ended in failure, as Confederate general Robert E. Lee kept McClellan away from Richmond—with a much smaller army than McClellan's. Lincoln replaced McClellan with John Pope. But Pope's army met defeat at Manassas, Virginia, in the second battle of Bull Run.

As Lee headed north, Lincoln put McClellan in charge of defending Washington, D.C. Finally, in September, Lincoln and McClellan got lucky. When Confederate orders fell into Union

The Battle of Antietam resulted in four thousand deaths in a single day.

hands, the Union army was able to block Lee's progress at Antietam, Maryland. The Battle of Antietam, September 17, 1862, which resulted in over four thousand deaths, is the deadliest single day in American history. But when it was through McClellan had turned Lee back, and Lincoln had the victory he needed.

The Emancipation Proclamation

On September 22, 1862, Lincoln presented his Emancipation Proclamation, which states that:

> *On the first day of January, in the year of our Lord, one thousand eight hundred and sixty three, all persons held as slaves within any State or designated part of a State, the people where of shall then be in rebellion against the United States, shall be then, thenceforward, and forever free.*

Like the title itself, the Emancipation Proclamation is formal and unemotional in tone. Lincoln used this tone to present emancipation as a thoughtful, strategic attempt to save the Union and end the war, not the passionate act of an abolitionist.

Technically, the Emancipation Proclamation didn't free a single slave. It granted freedom to slaves in Southern states over which the Union had no control—and even those states would be exempt if they rejoined the Union by the new year. It didn't even mention slavery in the states not "in rebellion"—the four border states.

But even with its limitations, the document was significant. It was the first time a president of the United States had granted freedom to slaves. In the eyes of people everywhere, it changed the meaning of the Civil War, making it a war about setting people free. In cities throughout the North supporters of the proclamation celebrated with rallies, parades, and bonfires. As New England authors praised Lincoln eloquently, others expressed their thanks in any way they could—a man from Baltimore sent Lincoln a half dozen hams. Lincoln himself thought the

African Americans celebrate the abolition of slavery in Washington, D.C.

Emancipation Proclamation was the one act for which he would be remembered.

While many cheered the proclamation, even some of Lincoln's greatest supporters resented his next action. On September 24, Lincoln limited certain rights to free speech throughout the land for the rest of the war. Now, simply for speaking out against the draft, a citizen could be arrested and put in jail without a trial. Lincoln insisted this emergency measure was necessary if the Union was to win the war. But many

Northerners began to share the Southern sentiment that Lincoln was becoming a tyrant.

Dissent in the Ranks

The 1862 elections went badly for Republicans. Democrats nearly overtook Congress—which was amazing, since only two years earlier half of their members had departed for the Confederacy. Republicans resented the political price they were paying for the unpopular president and his war.

With the president's popularity low, other Republicans tried to grab power. In the cabinet there was a sort of civil war between Seward and Chase that would become known as the Cabinet Crisis of '62. Besides having different political views, Seward and Chase had intense personalities and didn't like each other. When Chase complained to Congress that Seward had too much influence on the president, radicals in Congress began plotting to have Seward removed from his position. As the tension increased, both Seward and Chase threatened to resign. But Lincoln combined charm and toughness in dealing with their complaints head-on. He compelled both Chase and Seward to stay, showing them and Congress that he was still in control.

While staving off one mutiny in the cabinet, Lincoln had reason to fear another mutiny in the army. Like many of his officers, George McClellan tended to oppose emancipation. Thus, when the victorious general failed to pursue Confederate troops after the Battle of Antietam, Lincoln began to wonder if McClellan was trying to keep the North from winning the war.

Sensing Lincoln's mistrust, McClellan in turn became suspicious that the president was going to replace him. So McClellan sent the army's top spy, Allan Pinkerton, to meet with the president. Though Pinkerton had been sent to find out Lincoln's true feelings, it was Lincoln who used the meeting with Pinkerton to find out about McClellan. By asking a few subtle questions, Lincoln was able to confirm his suspicion that while the Battle of Antietam had been a Union victory, it had also been a wasted opportunity to crush the Confederacy for good.

So Lincoln replaced McClellan again, this time with Ambrose Burnside. Burnside has made a lasting impression in the world of fashion because of his large sideburns, the strips of facial hair which are named after him. But the impression he made on the country that December was not good. In the first major battle under Burnside's command, at Fredericksburg, Virginia, the Union suffered a devastating defeat.

In spite of countless military and political defeats, Lincoln continued to push for the causes in which he believed. Near the end of the year he addressed Congress to urge the passage of broader laws freeing the slaves. "[W]e cannot escape history," he insisted. "In giving freedom to the slave, we assure freedom to the free." As he built toward his finish, Lincoln warned, "We shall nobly save, or meanly lose, the last, best hope of earth."

This warning was not just rhetoric. Though Lincoln had raised the stakes by making the war about freedom as well as saving the Union, all his noble goals would be meaningless if he couldn't find a way to win the war.

A Perversion of History

On New Year's Day of 1863 the Emancipation Proclamation took effect, and Confederate slaves were given a new inspiration to flee their masters. Then Lincoln gave them yet another reason to flee: not only would they find freedom waiting in the north, they would find rifles.

Arming African Americans

Abolitionists had been urging Lincoln to allow blacks to enlist in the army since the beginning of the war. African-American spokesman Frederick Douglass demanded it. "Let the slaves and free colored people be called into service," he urged the president, "and formed into a liberating army."

Though the North certainly needed more troops, Lincoln worried that allowing former slaves to fight would upset Northern conservatives and make Southern whites so angry they'd never return to the Union. But in early 1863, he began to come around. By the spring, Lincoln was calling for massive recruitment of black troops.

Not surprisingly, Southerners despised Lincoln's decision to allow former slaves to be armed. Jefferson Davis announced that black Union soldiers who were captured would be enslaved. Other Confederate leaders threatened that they would be executed. In spite of this threat, blacks fought bravely and in great numbers. Eventually, an estimated 180,000 escaped slaves and

African-American men fought for the Union, risking their lives for the cause of freedom.

free blacks fought in the Union army and navy. The North could not have won without them.

As Lincoln had feared, his decision to allow blacks to enlist was unpopular with many in the North was well as in the South. To Northern Democrats it seemed that while Lincoln was empowering black people, he was stripping away the rights of white people. On April 13 Lincoln placed a new restriction on his citizens; now someone suspected of helping the Confederacy in any way could be arrested on the spot.

In response, Democratic Ohio congressman Clement Vallandigham called the president "King Lincoln" and demanded that a European nation step in to force Lincoln to negotiate a settlement to the war. When Vallandigham was arrested for these statements, there was an uproar among Democrats. Lincoln eventually had the congressman released from prison and exiled to the Confederacy. In protest, Ohio Democrats nominated Vallandigham for governor.

In the west, frustration with Lincoln and the war led to outbreaks of violence. One source of this frustration was the economy. While the war was creating jobs in the east, where factories produced weapons and military supplies, there were no similar benefits for westerners. Out of work and angry, many of these men had no interest in fighting to free slaves.

THE TIDE OF WAR

Lincoln believed his distressed citizens would be calmed if only the Union army could turn the tide and begin winning the war. But the tide didn't seem to be turning. Lincoln replaced Burnside with Joseph Hooker, but this general, too, oversaw a major defeat for the Union, in the Virginia town of Chancellorsville.

Grant's troops were struggling as well, as they tried to reach Vicksburg, Mississippi. If Grant could take Vicksburg, the Union would control the Mississippi River, which ran right down the middle of the Confederacy. In his desperation to get across the mighty river to Vicksburg, Grant had tried everything—even having his men dig trenches to reroute the flow of the river. But after months of men digging in the mud, the canal fell apart. Then Lincoln stopped hearing any news at all from Grant; it was as though the general and his men had just disappeared.

This mysterious news blackout in the west was accompanied by frightening news in the east: no longer contented to defend the Confederacy, Lee's armies were heading north, moving through Maryland and into the heart of the Union. Lincoln replaced Hooker with George Meade, and gave Meade the tall order of stopping the ingenious, daring Lee.

As the Union struggled on both fronts, observers found Lincoln especially tense. One visitor noted that Lincoln looked exhausted and weak, and that his hand trembled. "The president never tells a joke now," observed another.

Lincoln could get little cheer from his wife, who was still overwhelmed by grief. Over a year after Willie's death, Mary continued to wear black every day. She also held séances in the White House, believing she could make contact with her lost son. "Willie lives," she told one of her sisters. "He comes to me every night and stands at the foot of the bed with the same sweet adorable smile."

In early July Lincoln received incredible news: Meade had defeated Lee at Gettysburg, Pennsylvania. During three days of ferocious fighting, 23,000 Union soldiers had been killed, wounded, or captured, while Confederate casualties numbered 24,000. The day after learning about Gettysburg, Lincoln got more good news: Grant had taken Vicksburg. The general had been unable to communicate with Lincoln because he had crossed enemy lines to sneak up on Vicksburg from behind. With Grant's stunning victory, 29,000 confederate troops surrendered.

Vicksburg brought the Union a lasting breakthrough; with the Mississippi under Union control, the Confederacy was permanently split in half. But the victory at Gettysburg was followed by crushing disappointment for Lincoln. A few days after the battle he was horrified to learn that Meade had allowed Lee's troops to escape back to the Confederacy. "If I had gone up there I could have whipped them myself!" Lincoln lamented through tears to

Grant's relentless siege of Vicksburg lasted three days.

his son. More composed but still furious, Lincoln explained his anger to Meade in a letter he never sent:

> *My dear general, I do not believe you appreciate the magnitude of the misfortune involved in Lee's escape. He was within your easy grasp, and to have closed upon him would . . . have ended the war. As it is, the war will be prolonged indefinitely. . . . Your golden opportunity is gone, and I am distressed immeasurably because of it.*

Lincoln wasn't the only one getting restless. On July 13 riots erupted in New York. As in the west, this outbreak began among working-class whites who felt it was unfair that they had to be drafted to fight to free black people. Reckless mobs charged through the streets burning buildings, looting stores, and killing over a hundred people. Eventually Union troops had to be brought in to restore order.

For almost any other president, an episode like the New York draft riots would have been the administration's main crisis. For Lincoln it was a drop in the bucket. He did his best to downplay the horrifying violence rather than confront it directly and risk inspiring similar outbreaks across the North. "One rebellion at a time is about as much as we can conveniently handle," he concluded.

Rioters took to the streets of New York on July 13, 1863, in protest of the draft.

Addressing the People

As some Northerners rioted against the war and others simply complained, Lincoln longed to address the public directly. He wanted to help people understand the importance of the sacrifices they were being asked to make, to portray the war in a way that would reach their hearts and minds.

In Lincoln's day the president had few opportunities to speak directly to the people. There were no press conferences or public interviews. The president was expected to express his thoughts to Congress, or his cabinet, or other government officials, and then return to his office.

Lincoln found one opportunity to address the public directly when a group of New York Democrats led by Erastus Corning met to protest the arrest of Vallandigham. In response, Lincoln addressed to Corning a letter in which he carefully explained the extreme measures he was taking to protect public safety. The rebellion created an emergency situation, Lincoln claimed, in which defiant outcries like Vallandigham's call to abandon the war posed a threat to the Union. "Must I shoot a simple-minded soldier boy who deserts," Lincoln asked, "while I must not touch a hair of a wiley agitator who induces him to desert?"

Lincoln's Letter to Corning was mailed to politicians, published in newspapers, released as a pamphlet, and read by over ten million people. The response was overwhelmingly positive. Through his persuasive published speech, the president was able to convince people that "King Lincoln" had in fact only been doing his job.

Another opportunity to address the public came in September, when Congressman James C. Conkling invited Lincoln to

MY FRIEND DOUGLASS

Abolitionists were known for their hatred of slavery. But abolitionist Frederick Douglass spoke against slavery with a passion that was particularly inspired, since he had been a slave himself. Born into slavery in Maryland, Douglass was taught to read by his master's wife and learned to write through his own efforts. As a young man Douglass escaped to freedom in the north, where he immediately began spreading the word about the horrors he had witnessed.

"My mother and I were separated when I was but an infant," Douglass wrote in *The Narrative of the Life of Frederick Douglass*. The book goes on to describe how slaves were routinely raped, humiliated, and whipped until blood poured down their backs. His antislavery speeches, as powerful as his writings, earned Douglass a key position in the abolitionist movement.

Eventually recognized as the leading spokesman for African Americans, Douglass met with Lincoln several times to discuss issues involving freedom for slaves and equal rights for African Americans. The two men quickly developed a cordial working relationship, with Lincoln referring to Douglass as "my friend Douglass," and Douglass praising Lincoln for being the first American official he met who had no racial prejudice.

Like all abolitionists, Douglass was often frustrated by Lincoln's slowness to act on behalf of slaves and African Americans. Looking back, Douglass claimed that Lincoln was "the white man's president, entirely devoted to the welfare of white men." But he went on to explain that Lincoln's attention to white voters proved to be "one element of his wonderful success" bringing the country "safely through the conflict" which brought slavery to an end.

After Lincoln's presidency, Douglass continued to write and speak out for equal rights for African Americans, and for women as well. He served in a series of government positions, including U.S. ambassador to Haiti.

speak at a Republican rally in Illinois. Though Lincoln couldn't attend, he sent a letter in which he tried to inspire support for the war. Realizing that opinion about the Emancipation Proclamation was divided, Lincoln addressed people on both sides of the issue. Those who believed in emancipation should fight to free the slaves, Lincoln urged. Those who didn't care for emancipation should fight to save the Union—and realize that black soldiers were fighting to help achieve that goal. Trying to change the minds of whites who resented emancipation, Lincoln predicted that when the war was over there would be "some black men who can remember that, with silent tongue, and clenched teeth, and steady eye, and well-poised bayonnet, they have helped mankind."

Read aloud at the rally, Lincoln's "Conkling Letter" was cheered by a crowd of thousands. Then it was published in newspapers across the country and widely praised. Once again, Lincoln had been able to craft a speech that helped Americans to understand his vision.

But he still hadn't reached the public with the exact message he wanted to send. He wanted the people to see the conflict as a people's war. He wanted to convince people that the ideas of Union and freedom are linked. The chance to share that vision finally came, when organizers of a ceremony in Gettysburg invited Lincoln to attend and make "a few appropriate remarks."

THE GETTYSBURG ADDRESS

On November 19, 1863, some 20,000 people gathered on a field in Gettysburg, Pennsylvania. For the past four months workers had been burying the dead left by the previous summer's notoriously deadly battle. Now Americans were anxious to dedicate the new cemetery as a way of mourning and honoring the thousands of fallen men.

The afternoon's main speaker, Edward Everett of Massachusetts, gave a detailed description of the battle in a speech that lasted about two hours. Lincoln followed Everett, delivering a speech that lasted only two minutes. But the president's brief speech at Gettysburg is now considered one of the most powerful ever made. In the words of historian Garry Wills, the Gettysburg Address "remade America."

As striking as what Lincoln said at Gettysburg is what he didn't say. He didn't mention a single soldier by name. He didn't use the words North or South, black or white, or even the word Gettysburg. Instead, he described the conflict in an abstract way, boiling it down to what he considered its most basic elements:

Four score and seven years ago our fathers brought forth on this continent a new nation, conceived in Liberty, and dedicated to the proposition that all men are created equal.

Lincoln started by claiming that the nation had begun eighty-seven years earlier, in 1776, with the signing of the Declaration of Independence. (Since a "score" is twenty, four score plus seven is

At the dedication of the Gettysburg National Cemetary Lincoln delivered a brief address that changed the nation.

eighty-seven.) Many Americans felt the nation began more recently, with the **Constitution**, which emphasized the power of the states and allowed slavery. But Lincoln had always preferred the Declaration, which suggests that the colonies were linked from the start by a "self-evident truth" that "all men are created equal."

"Now we are engaged in a great civil war," Lincoln continued, "testing whether that nation, or any nation so conceived and so dedicated can long endure." In this second sentence, Lincoln described the war as a test in which Union soldiers were trying to prove that a nation devoted to equal rights could survive.

After praising the bravery of the men who fell, Lincoln looked to the future, urging:

> That from these honored dead we take increased devotion to that cause for which they gave their last full measure of devotion—that we here highly resolve that these dead shall not have died in vain; that this nation, under God, shall have a new birth of freedom; and that government of the people, by the people, for the people shall not perish from the earth.

With this rousing call to action, the Gettysburg Address ended. Direct and clear, the speech expressed complex thoughts and feelings Lincoln had been grappling with for years. And all in ten sentences.

The *Chicago Times* called Lincoln's speech a "perversion of history" in which the president lied about the cause for which the nation was founded and the Civil War fought. "How dared he," the paper railed, "standing on their graves, misstate the cause for which they died and libel the statesmen who founded the government?"

In a sense this criticism was valid. Opposition to slavery motivated only some of the Union soldiers, as it had motivated only some of the nation's founders. Though the United States had been founded in the name of liberty, there had always been disagreement about who was entitled to enjoy that liberty, and whether states were at liberty to leave. Uncertain of its focus, the nation was like a party in which guests disagreed about what was being celebrated, or a game in which players disagreed about the goal.

In the Gettysburg Address, Lincoln aimed to end that uncertainty. Instead of describing the nation, he set out to define it. According to Lincoln's definition, the United States always had been, and always would be, a unified nation devoted to the concept of equal rights. Lincoln took his version of the truth to the audience at Gettysburg and tried to sell it as fact.

And it worked. While some newspaper editors were appalled, many more were impressed with the simple power and beauty of Lincoln's message. Those in attendance were thrilled as well, interrupting the speech five times with bursts of applause. They departed from Gettysburg with a new sense of history, which would gradually come to be accepted throughout the land.

"Lincoln had revolutionized the Revolution," Wills explains, "giving people a new past to live with that would change their future indefinitely." In a series of careful steps, Lincoln had transformed the Civil War from a domestic dispute into a contest to see whether lasting freedom was possible on earth.

CHEW AND CHOKE

Six

Over the first three years of his term Lincoln feared his power might be undermined by **treason**, sabotage, and spying. But in the fourth year Lincoln began to fear that all he had tried to achieve might be undone by something that was completely legal: an election.

COUNTING ON GRANT

As the election of 1864 approached, Lincoln realized that voters would reelect him only if they felt the war was going well. For this reason the president was counting on General Grant to help secure victory at the polls as well as on the battlefield. In Grant, Lincoln had finally found a general he could work with. Grant never shied away from conflict or let an enemy escape. "Unconditional Surrender" Grant, as he was called, was committed to Lincoln's belief that the war must be won by any means necessary.

As Grant continued to win battles in the west, Lincoln wanted to promote Grant to put him in charge of the entire **Union** army. But these victories were making the general so popular Lincoln feared Grant might run for president himself. So Lincoln had a mutual friend ask Grant about his political intentions, and was relieved to hear that Grant had none.

In March, Lincoln summoned Grant to the White House to make Grant the first five-star general since George Washington. After formal ceremonies, Lincoln and Grant strategized together, planning to attack the Confederacy on all fronts at once. As Grant would lead troops toward the Confederate capital of

76

Lincoln's five-star general Ulysses S. Grant stands (center) with his Civil War staff.

Richmond, General William Tecumseh Sherman would march from Tennessee to Atlanta, Georgia, and then to the sea. With Grant overseeing the war, Lincoln could focus on the election.

RENOMINATION

As his first step toward reelection, Lincoln needed to be nominated by his party. But the Republican Party was in flux. Aiming to put partisanship aside during wartime, many Republicans teamed up with Democrats who supported the war to form the Union Party. A group of Radical Republicans, however, were

THE SENSITIVE WAR PRESIDENT

The Civil War was by far the nation's bloodiest, resulting in over a half million American deaths. And yet the president who steered the nation through this brutal war was unusually sensitive to suffering. On his frequent visits to Union hospitals, Lincoln seemed to observers to feel personally responsible for each casualty. Lincoln himself was perplexed by the fact that as someone who "couldn't cut off the head of a chicken, or stand the sight of blood," he should have anything to do with mass slaughter.

Compelling evidence of Lincoln's sensitivity can be found in the letters he wrote to relatives of fallen soldiers. To Fanny McCullough, a young person whose father was killed in battle, Lincoln wrote:

Dear Fanny,

It is with deep grief that I learn of the death of your kind and brave Father; and, especially, that it is affecting your heart beyond what is common in such cases. In this sad world of ours, sorrow comes to all; and, to the young, it comes with bitterest agony, because it takes them unawares. The older have learned ever to expect it. I am anxious to afford some alleviation of your present distress. Perfect relief is not possible, except with time. You can not now realize that you will ever feel better. Is not this so? And yet it is a mistake. You are sure to be happy again. To know this, which is certainly true, will make you some less miserable now. I have had experience enough to know what I say; and you need only to believe it, to feel better at once. The memory of your dear Father, instead of an agony, will yet be a sad sweet feeling in your heart, of a purer, and holier sort than you have known before. Please present my kind regards to your afflicted mother.

Your sincere friend,
A. Lincoln

unwilling to team up with Democrats. Instead they formed their own party and chose General Frémont as their candidate.

Though the Radical Republicans were convinced Lincoln couldn't possibly be reelected, members of the Union Party felt otherwise. They chose Lincoln as their nominee, with Democratic senator Andrew Johnson of Tennessee as the candidate for vice president. In accepting the Union Party's nomination, Lincoln offered an anecdote to discourage voters from changing presidents during a war: "I am reminded . . . of a story of an old Dutch farmer," Lincoln said, "who remarked to a companion once that it was not best to swap horses when crossing streams."

The Democrats, however, were quite anxious to swap horses. As their candidate they chose General McClellan, who promised that if Southerners would surrender, they could keep their slaves. This position was a striking contrast to that held by Lincoln, who now demanded an end to slavery as a condition for surrender.

A FIGHT TO THE FINISH

With the political battle lines drawn, campaigners went to battle. McClellan supporters called Lincoln a tyrant, a fanatic, a buffoon, and "Ignoramus Abe." Lincoln supporters called McClellan a coward and a defeatist; some even accused him of treason.

Some of Lincoln's advisers urged the president to postpone the election until the war was over. No nation had ever held an election in the middle of a major war. But Lincoln felt the country had to face the test. As he would later explain,

This political cartoon from the 1864 presidential election contrasts Lincoln's attitude toward slavery with McClellan's.

> *We cannot have free government without elections, and if the rebellion could force us to forego, or postpone a national election, it might fairly claim to have already conquered and ruined us.*

Over the course of the campaign, Lincoln had reason to wish he'd decided otherwise. In Virginia, Grant and Lee were locked in a deadly stalemate. In the Battle of the Wilderness, and other horrific engagements in Spotsylvania and Cold Harbor, both sides suffered staggering losses. By July over 100,000 Union soldiers had been killed or wounded in six weeks. Though the press called Grant a butcher and urged his removal, Lincoln stuck with his general. "Hold on with a bull dog grip," he urged Grant, "and chew and choke as much as possible." But victory continued to elude Grant, and Lincoln's popularity continued to sink.

Eventually Lincoln became convinced he would lose the election. In despair, he wrote a memo to members of his cabinet, which read:

This morning, as for some days past, it seems exceedingly probable that this administration will not be re-elected. Then it will be my duty to so co-operate with the President elect, as to save the Union between the election and inauguration; as he will have secured his election on such ground that he can not possibly save it afterwards.

Though he decided to keep the memo's contents to himself, Lincoln foresaw a dire situation: if McClellan won the election, Lincoln would have only four months to win the war, save the Union, and end slavery—or everything he had fought for would be lost.

Then, on September 4, Lincoln received stunning news: Sherman had captured Atlanta. With the Deep South opening up and Grant continuing to wear down Lee, Union victory seemed within grasp. As Republicans

When this photo was taken, Lincoln was trying to win an election and a war.

pulled together behind Lincoln, Frémont dropped out of the race. On election day voters rewarded Lincoln for his success as a wartime leader. "Long Abe Lincoln a little longer!" one newspaper announced. Lincoln won a landslide victory.

BITTER LOSERS

Some Southerners were so infuriated by Lincoln's continued success that they resorted to desperate measures. A Confederate minister came north hoping to kidnap Lincoln, bring him to Confederate territory, and force the Union to negotiate a peace settlement. Though this minister and his team of kidnappers spent months stalking the president, they never found the right moment to seize him.

Another plot against Lincoln came closer to success: a would-be assassin fired a shot at the president, blasting a hole in Lincoln's top hat. Luckily for the president the horse upon which he was sitting was startled by the noise and galloped away, robbing the gunman of another clear shot. Aware that more plots were being hatched, Lincoln kept eighty letters containing threats on his life stashed away in his desk. "I know I am in danger," Lincoln confided to a reporter, "but I am not going to worry over threats like these."

LOOKING AHEAD

With the election over, Lincoln began to look ahead to his second term. In particular he devoted time to planning reconstruction, the process of bringing the Southern states back into the Union after the war. Lincoln proposed a plan to Congress, by which Southerners who promised to be loyal to the Union would be forgiven for their past rebellious actions. While this aspect of Lin-

In capturing Atlanta, General Sherman left the city's transportation system and many buildings in ruins.

coln's plan pleased Democrats, another aspect of the plan pleased radicals: it outlawed slavery.

As Lincoln planned to end slavery in the South, he finally felt he had enough political power to end slavery in the border states. Under Lincoln's guidance, Congress passed the Thirteenth Amendment to the Constitution, which outlawed slavery, permanently, throughout the country.

Lincoln had come a long way from his first day as president when he had promised not to disturb slavery, to the brink of outlawing it completely. But this one-step-at-a-time process for facing a crisis was not new to Lincoln. When the young Lincoln and his family had arrived in the Indiana wilderness in the dead of winter, they built a half-faced camp—three walls, a roof, and a fire. That precarious shack was an uncomfortable place to stay, but it kept the Lincolns alive through the night and bought them time to build a more stable structure. Similarly, when Lincoln found himself at the helm of a nation in crisis, he tolerated slavery where it already existed to appease slaveholders. Then he offered limited freedom with the Emancipation Proclamation. Over time he was able to build onto these temporary measures, until he felt the nation was ready for lasting freedom.

As Lincoln began his second term, all that stood between him and his goal—a nation united without slavery—was that final military victory.

With the Civil War apparently in its final stages, Lincoln dreaded the possibility of a stalemate. Though the Confederates were clearly losing, they still might be able to avoid capture and wear down Union troops, forcing a compromise. Lincoln was determined to see that the Union victory was decisive, so there would be no compromise on the issues for which the war was being fought.

Early in 1865 Lincoln received unofficial requests from the Confederacy to discuss peace plans. In response to one of these Lincoln agreed to meet informally with Confederate vice president Alexander Stephens on a steamboat. Lincoln and Stephens had been Whigs in Congress together, so their conversation was friendly. But it was also fruitless. Lincoln made it clear that he would never recognize the Confederacy as a separate nation. He would never have an official meeting with the Confederate president. He would never negotiate with the rebels until they laid down their weapons. So there was no laying down of weapons, and war continued.

THE SECOND INAUGURATION

On March 4 Lincoln delivered his second inaugural address to the nation. He devoted a large portion of the brief speech to a summary of the war, in which he took pains to present people on both sides as human:

Both read the same Bible, and pray to the same God; and each invokes His aid against the Other . . . the prayers of both could not be answered.

Though the two sides had been slaughtering hundreds of thousands of each other's young men, Lincoln managed to describe the war almost as though it was no one's fault; it had been inevitable. At the same time, he made it clear that he would pursue the war as long as it took for the Union to win.

In closing, Lincoln looked from the terrible war to the peace that would follow, and the need to repair the nation in a spirit of forgiveness.

With malice toward none; with charity for all; with firmness in the right, as God gives us to see the right, let us strive on to finish the work we are in; to bind up the nation's wounds; to care for him who shall have borne the battle, and for his widow, and his orphan—to do all which may achieve and cherish a just, and a lasting peace, among ourselves, and with all nations.

As Lincoln spoke of binding wounds, the effects of the mental suffering he himself had endured were evident on his face. Photographs taken at the time of his second inauguration reveal dark circles around his eyes and deep creases all over his face that made him look as though he had aged far more than four years since his first inauguration.

Lincoln was in fact profoundly exhausted. Mary Lincoln feared he wouldn't live out the term. And even with the war winding down he continued to worry, obsessed that military victory would somehow slip through his fingers.

This photo of Lincoln, taken four days before his death, reveals wrinkles and creases caused by his stressful years in office.

VICTORY

On March 20 Lincoln visited Grant's headquarters at City Point, Virginia, to see for himself how things were going. When Lincoln's generals assured him the Confederacy was about to crumble, the president urged them not to become overconfident.

But their confidence was justified. Shortly after Lincoln's visit, Richmond fell to Union troops. With the Confederate capital taken, President Jefferson Davis fled. When Lincoln came to Richmond and walked through the streets, bitter Southern whites ignored him, but freed slaves recognized him and cheered "Glory hallelujah!" In a moment of symbolic importance, Lincoln entered the capitol and sat in Jefferson Davis's chair.

Even at this point, Lincoln continued to worry about the war's outcome. He feared that if the Union didn't receive a formal surrender from the Confederacy in the next few days, there might soon be no one left with whom to negotiate. This could result in various armed bands of rebels throughout the south, and drawn out violence and conflict.

On April 9, at long last, the Civil War came to its official end, as Lee surrendered to Grant in Appomattox Courthouse in Virginia. Grant offered the Confederate soldiers generous terms: after turning in their weapons they could return home; and they could keep their horses, which they would need for farming. People on both sides were relieved that the end was within sight.

AFTER THE WAR

Throughout the North people celebrated by waving flags, ringing bells, and dancing in the streets. Outside the White House

Jubilant freed slaves greet Lincoln on his visit to Richmond.

crowds gathered to call for the president. Lincoln finally appeared
at a window, but he refused to give a speech. Instead he asked
the White House band to honor the former enemy by playing the
Southern anthem "Dixie," which Lincoln called "one of the best

tunes I have ever heard." Lincoln appeared at the window, waving a Confederate flag.

But two days later, when another jubilant crowd arrived outside his window, Lincoln did have a speech to deliver. Turning to the question of rebuilding the nation, Lincoln discussed his plan for bringing Southern states back to their "proper practical relation" with the Union. In this speech Lincoln revealed that he intended to approach reconstruction as he had emancipation: one step at a time. As one of these steps Lincoln proposed that some freed slaves be allowed to vote.

Lincoln was trying to present his plan as moderate and gradual to avoid sparking anger. But one listener in the crowd outside his window was infuriated. A twenty-six-year-old actor who belonged to a famous theatrical family, John Wilkes Booth was a Marylander who sympathized with the Confederate cause. The previous year he had plotted to kidnap Lincoln. But now, hearing Lincoln suggest that blacks be allowed to vote, Booth decided more drastic measures had to be taken. "That is the last speech he will ever make," Booth vowed. With a group of conspirators, Booth plotted to murder the president and other leaders in hopes of throwing the government into chaos.

Meanwhile, Lincoln was looking to the future. He devised a plan to pay off the nation's enormous war debt with gold to be found in California and other western states. He looked forward to the end of his term, when he would visit Europe, and move back to Illinois. Above all, he looked forward to being happy. "We must both be more cheerful in the future," he told Mary while on an afternoon carriage ride. "[B]etween the war and the loss of our darling Willie we have both been miserable."

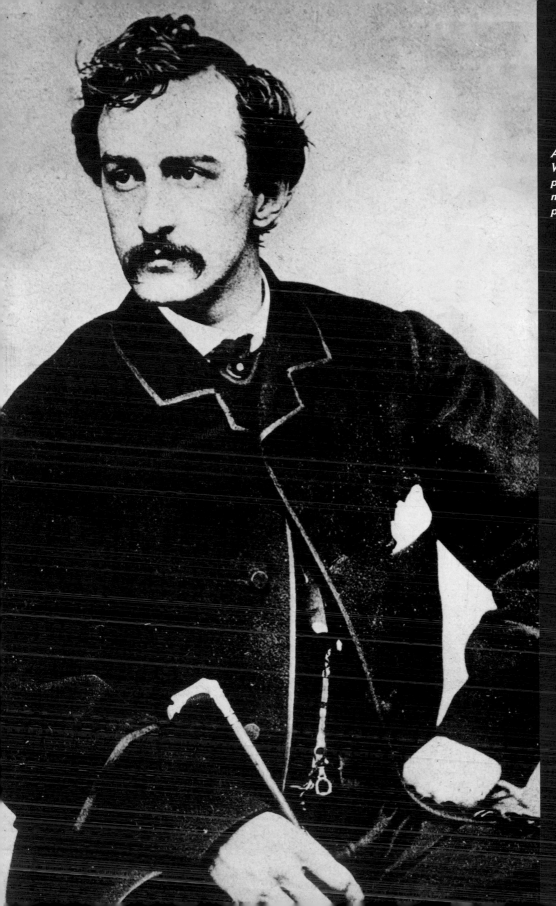

ASSASSINATION

On the evening of April 14 the first couple went to see a comedy called *Our American Cousin* at Ford's Theater. When the Lincolns arrived in their balcony seats the entire packed house gave the president a standing ovation. During the performance observers noted that the Lincolns were holding hands, laughing, and speaking softly to one another.

Meanwhile, Booth slipped into the presidential box bearing a concealed pistol. To get by a guard, the actor had presented a card proving his involvement in the theater. As Lincoln watched the play, Booth watched Lincoln from a few feet away.

During the laughter following a comic line in the third act, a shot rang out. Booth leapt from the balcony to the stage and shouted *"Sic semper tyrannis!"*—Latin for "So it always is for tyrants!"—before dashing away. Audience members thought Booth's sudden appearance was part of the play until they heard Mary Lincoln scream out, "They have shot the president!" Lincoln had been hit just behind the left ear.

The unconscious president was rushed to a nearby house where several doctors and government officials assembled. When it became clear that the president's life could not be saved, those in attendance watched and mourned. As the night progressed Lincoln's breathing became labored. At 7:22 on the morning of April 15, with Mary and Robert at his side, Abraham Lincoln died. Vice President Andrew Johnson became president as, for the first time, a president of the United States had been assassinated.

Of the team of assassins, only Booth accomplished his goal. The conspirator assigned to kill Johnson had changed his mind.

John Wilkes Booth shot President Abraham Lincoln as he and his wife watched a play at Ford's Theater in Washington, D.C.

Another member of Booth's team had attacked and nearly killed Seward. But successful or not, all conspirators were quickly rounded up. Booth was shot while resisting arrest. The rest were tried and hanged.

Lincoln's Legacy

No punishment, however, could compensate the nation for the loss of its president. Killed only one month into his second term, Lincoln would never get his chance to "bind up the nation's wounds."

The process of reconstruction proved more difficult than anyone could have imagined. As Northern politicians tried to empower Southern blacks, Southern whites became infuriated and responded with mob violence in terrorist groups such as the Ku Klux Klan. When reconstruction was finally cut short in 1876, African Americans in the South were forced to live as second-class citizens, in conditions not unlike those they had endured under slavery. Whether Lincoln would have done a better job of bringing whites and blacks together is uncertain. But his gift for uniting opposing groups of people was sorely missed.

Lincoln's popularity soared immediately after his death. Speakers compared him to such biblical figures as Moses. Painters portrayed him as a divine being. Even in the South Lincoln was remembered by some as a sympathetic leader who would have protected Southern whites from vengeful Northern politicians.

In the years to follow Lincoln became a symbol for the cause of freedom around the world. From Spain to South Africa to Vietnam to Communist China, people fighting for freedom would invoke the name and words of Abraham Lincoln. Most famously, Martin Luther King echoed Lincoln in 1963 when he stood on the steps of the Lincoln Memorial in Washington, D.C., and delivered his "I have a dream speech," which begins: "Five score years ago, a great American, in whose symbolic shadow we stand, signed the Emancipation Proclamation."

A hero to freedom fighters, Lincoln has been admired by most scholars—but not all. Well into the twentieth century some historians criticized Lincoln for assuming too much power and being too aggressive in his efforts to bring an end to slavery. More recently, some historians have criticized Lincoln for being too tolerant of slavery, suggesting that he took steps to end slavery only to preserve the Union.

But in the eyes of most historians, the simple facts of Abraham Lincoln's life are enough to earn him top ranking among American presidents. He came from poverty in the wilderness, taught himself to read and write, and speak and lead. Through four traumatic years he kept the country united, oversaw the outlawing of slavery, and gave the people a new sense of what it meant to be American.

The people of the United States continue to live by the principles of **democracy** as Lincoln interpreted them. Though there are disagreements about the limits of individual freedoms, the basic principle that human beings are entitled to equal rights is accepted across the land. And when Americans don't like the direction in which their country is going, they don't start a new country. They speak out, write letters, carry signs, create Web sites, have sit-ins, write songs, march . . . and vote. And people around the world have proof that a government controlled by "the people" can last.

Lincoln continues to inspire those who dream of freedom. But in May 1865 he mainly inspired grief. As his body was transported

THE LINCOLN FAMILY

Though Lincoln's oldest son, Robert, spent most of his father's presidency away at college, the younger boys, Willie and Tad, made the most of their time in the White House. When not romping with their pets—which included a pony and two goats—the rambunctious boys enjoyed the occasional romp with their fun-loving father. A pushover who left discipline to his wife, the president was known to devote brief breaks from work to rolling around on the floor with the boys.

But such times of family fun were few and far between for the Lincolns. Willie's death at age eleven, together with the prolonged war, caused both parents heartache.

While Booth's bullet ended the life of another Lincoln and ended the Lincolns' stay in the White House, it did not end the string of tragedies that plagued the family. Mary, who had been high-strung before, became obsessed with a fear of poverty and began selling her expensive dresses. When Tad died of tuberculosis at age eighteen, Mary's emotional instability increased. Eventually Robert, who had become a lawyer, began a legal proceeding to have his mother put in a mental hospital. Though Mary eventually was released from the hospital and was found to be sane, more misery and bad health awaited. She died at age sixty-four of an uncertain disease that left her partially paralyzed and blind.

Of all the Lincolns' children, only Robert lived to adulthood. Besides being a lawyer, he was a renowned businessman whose success overseeing the Pullman rail car company brought him great wealth. He also served as secretary of war under presidents James Garfield and Chester Arthur, and as ambassador to England under President Benjamin Harrison. Though often urged to run for president himself, he consistently refused, even becoming irritated by the suggestion. In 1922, four years before his death at the age of eighty-two, Robert Lincoln helped President Warren Harding dedicate the Lincoln Memorial.

from Washington, D.C., up the East Coast to New York and then westward for burial, millions came for a last look at the face of their fallen leader. They wept and called him Father Abraham, because in their time of chaos and crisis he had come to feel like a watchful parent who would somehow see them through. And so Lincoln's body was returned to its final resting place in Springfield, the town from which some four years earlier he had departed filled with fear and hope.

President Abraham Lincoln gave people a new sense of what it means to be American.

TIMELINE

1809
Born in Kentucky, February 12

1832
Runs for state legislature and loses

1834
Elected to the state legislature

1842
Marries Mary Todd

1846
Elected to the U.S. House of Representatives

1858
Runs for U.S. Senate and loses

1800

1860
Elected president

1863
Emancipation Proclamation
takes effect; Gettysburg
Address, November 19

1864
Reelected president

1865
Assassinated April 14

1865

GLOSSARY

abolitionist someone who believed slavery should be ended at once

border states during the Civil War, the four states in the Union where slavery remained legal: Kentucky, West Virginia, Missouri, and Maryland

Confederate States of America the new nation formed by southern states that left the Union

Congress the federal lawmaking body of the United States, comprised of the Senate and the House of Representatives

conservative opposed to change

Constitution the document that contains the basic laws and principles on which the United States is founded

democracy a government in which power is controlled by the people

emancipation the process of setting free

half-faced camp a temporary, hastily prepared wooden structure made up of three walls and a fire that burns night and day

House of Representatives the larger house of Congress to which representatives are elected to two year terms

inaugural address a speech given at a ceremony that celebrates the beginning of a term of office

radical favoring extreme actions

reconstruction the process of bringing the Confederate states back into the Union

secessionists people who believed a southern state should leave the Union

secretary of state the member of the president's cabinet responsible for over-seeing foreign affairs

Supreme Court the highest, most powerful court in the United States

state legislature a body of representatives responsible for lawmaking in a par-ticular state

treason trying to overthrow the government to which one owes loyalty

Union the body of states that were not in rebellion

Whigs members of an American political party formed in 1834

FURTHER INFORMATION

BOOKS

Aronson, Billy. *Ulysses S. Grant* (Presidents and Their Times). Tarrytown, NY: Marshall Cavendish Benchmark, 2008.

Howell, Maria, L. *The Emancipation Proclamation*. Farmington Hills, MI: Lucent Books, 2006.

Murray, Aaron R.,ed. *Cival War*. New York: Dorling Kindersley Publishing, 2004.

Taylor, Yuval. *Growing Up in Slavery: Stories of Young Slaves as Told by Themselves*. Chicago: Lawrence Hill Books, 2005.

DVDs

A & E Home Video. *The Civil War*, 2007.
PBS Paramount. *Abraham and Mary Lincoln: A House Divided*, 2005.

WEB SITES

The Last Full Measure: Abraham Lincoln 1809–1865

www.thelastfullmeasure.com

This Web site features Lincoln's greatest speeches, selected letters, and an account of his life written by Lincoln himself.

Lincoln Home National Historic Site

www.nps.gov/liho

This site offers a tour of Lincoln's home in Springfield, and provides links to essays and poems about Lincoln, quotes from Lincoln on various issues, and the complete transcripts of the Lincoln–Douglas debates.

Abraham Lincoln Papers at the Library of Congress

www.memory.loc.gov/ammem/alhtml/malhome.html

Thousands of images of actual historic documents, including letters and notes by and to Lincoln and drafts of his speeches.

BIBLIOGRAPHY

Angle, Paul M. *The Lincoln Reader*. New York: Da Capo Press, 1947.

Boller, Paul F. Jr. *Presidential Campaigns*. New York: Oxford University Press, 1984.

Dole, Bob. *Great Presidential Wit*. New York: Charles Scribner's Sons, 2001.

Donald, David Herbert. *Lincoln*. New York: Touchstone Books, 1995.

Gienapp, William E. *This Fiery Trial: The Speeches and Writings of Abraham Lincoln*. Oxford, England: Oxford University Press, 2002.

Holzer, Harold. *Lincoln as I Knew Him*. New York: Workman
Publishing, 1999.

Mitgang, Herbert. *Abraham Lincoln: A Press Portrait*. Athens:
University of Georgia Press, 1956.

Wills, Garry. *Lincoln at Gettysburg*. New York: Simon & Schuster,
Inc., 1992.

Wead, Doug. *All the President's Children*. New York: Atria Books,
2003.

Wilson, Edmund. *Patriotic Gore*. Oxford, England: Oxford University
Press, 1962.

INDEX

Pages in **boldface** are illustrations.

★ ★ ★ ★ ★ ★ ★ ★ ★ ★ ★ ★ ★ ★ ★ ★ ★

ABOUT THE AUTHOR

Billy Aronson's plays have been produced by Playwrights Horizons, Ensemble Studio Theatre, Woolly Mammoth Theatre, and Wellfleet Harbor Actor's Theatre, published in *Best American Short Plays*, and awarded a New York Foundation for the Arts grant. His TV writing includes scripts for *Courage the Cowardly Dog*, *Beavis & Butt-head*, *The Wonder Pets* (head writer first season), *Postcards from Buster* (Emmy Nomination), *The Upside Down Show*, and *Johnny and the Sprites*. His writing for the musical theater includes the original concept and additional lyrics for the Broadway musical *Rent*. He wrote *Ulysses S. Grant* and *Richard M. Nixon* for the Marshall Cavendish series Presidents and Their Times. He lives in Brooklyn with his wife, Lisa Vogel, and their children, Jake and Anna. For more on Aronson, visit billyaronson.com.